What Does An Angel Look Like?

Six Meditations

on Christmas

By Joshua Brown

Published by Good Read Press
450 College Avenue, Richmond, IN 47374

What Does An Angel Look Like? Six Meditations on Christmas
Copyright © 2000 by Joshua Brown

All rights reserved. No part of this book may be reproduced in any form or by any electronic or mechanical means including information storage and retrieval systems without written permission from the publisher. Reviewers may quote brief passages to be printed in a magazine or newspaper.

Library of Congress Number: 00-191017
ISBN: 0-9674173-2-5

Revised Standard Version of the Bible, 2nd edition copyright 1971 by the Division of Christian Education of the National Council of the Churches of Christ in the United States of America. Used by permission. All rights reserved. New Revised Standard Version Bible, copyright 1989, Division of Christian Education of the National Council of the Churches of Christ in the United States of America. Used by permission. All rights reserved.

Cover drawings by Norma Jacke Tucker. All rights reserved.

Table of Contents

	Before We Start i
I	Prepare Ye the Way 1
	Luke 3:1-18
II	What Does an Angel Look Like? 11
	Luke 1:5-38
III	Led By a Little Child 25
	Isaiah 11:1-9
IV	The Gift of Christmas 38
	Luke 2:1-20
V	Joseph, the Dreamer 48
	Matthew 1:18-2:23
VI	Questions 59
	Luke 2:41-52

Before We Start. . .

I love Christmas.

I love it in spite of everything we do to the holiday. Yes, I get tired of the mindless mall music, the never-ending TV specials, the advertising that starts in September, the frantic round of parties, and the rush to the stores again on December 26th.

We keep coming back to the Christmas story, because it speaks to our hearts and minds at the deepest level, and because it challenges us to look at the world in a different way.

What if we could strip all of the "extras" away? What if we could go back and hear the Christmas story for the first time?

Could the story have worked out in a different way? What would have happened if Mary had said, "No!"? Do we hear what the prophets were really saying? What happens when Christmas Day is over and we have to go on with our lives?

It's been 2,000 years, more or less, since the angels sang, "Glory to God in the highest! Peace on earth, good will to all people!" And we are still hungry for glory, peace and love.

These meditations are my attempt to walk through the Christmas story with fresh eyes and ears. I want to try to see the people as real human beings like me, not as two-dimensional characters following a script.

May these meditations help you, as they have helped me, to welcome the birth of Christ.

Joshua Brown
Richmond, Indiana

I

Prepare Ye the Way

Advent is a long season, during which we listen to all the stories, ponder their meaning, and wonder in our hearts whether we're really ready for the birth of Jesus, for the coming of the Savior.

Every year, I read this part of the Advent story – the story of John the Baptist, the cousin of Jesus, the one who was sent before Jesus to prepare the way. And every year, I wonder if I really understand it.

John the Baptist is an enigmatic figure whenever we meet him in the stories of the New Testament. We don't know very much about him. According to Jesus, John the Baptist was the greatest prophet since Elijah. In fact, according to Jesus, John *was* Elijah, returned to earth again.

More than any other person except Jesus himself, John gripped the imagination of the people of his time.

Ordinary people came by the thousands to listen to him. Kings and people of power feared him. And yet, we know very little about the mysterious figure of John. It's as if against the richer portrait of Jesus we're given in the gospels, John is only sketched for us in outline.

And maybe John himself would have wanted it that way. After all, didn't John say: "There is one coming after me, who is greater than I am. I am not even worthy to kneel down and untie the strap of his sandals. I baptize you with water, but the one who is coming after me will baptize you with the Holy Spirit, and with fire . . ."

The job of John the Baptist, as he saw it, was to *prepare* people for the coming of Christ. We read about John, at the beginning of Advent, to prepare ourselves for the coming of Jesus into the world.

Luke 3:1-18

In the fifteenth year of the reign of Tiberius Caesar, Pontius Pilate being governor of Judea, and Herod being tetrarch of Galilee, and his brother Philip tetrarch of the region of Ituraea and Trachonitis, and Lysanias tetrarch of Abilene, in the high-priesthood of Annas and Caiaphas, the word of God came to John the son of Zechariah in the wilderness; and he went into all the region about the Jordan, preaching a baptism of repentance for the forgiveness of sins.

As it is written in the book of the words of Isaiah the prophet, "The voice of one crying in the wilderness: Prepare the way of the Lord, make his paths straight. Every valley shall be filled, and every mountain and hill shall be brought low, and the crooked shall be made straight, and the rough ways shall be made smooth; and all flesh shall see the salvation of God."

He said therefore to the multitudes that came out to be baptized by him, "You brood of vipers! Who warned you to flee from the wrath to come? Bear fruits that befit repentance, and do not begin to say to yourselves, 'We have Abraham as our father'; for I tell you, God is able from these stones to raise up children to Abraham. Even now the axe is laid to the root of the trees; every tree therefore that does not bear good fruit is cut down and thrown into the fire."

And the multitudes asked him, "What then shall we do?"

And he answered them, "He who has two coats, let him share with him who has none; and he who has food, let him do likewise."

Tax collectors also came to be baptized, and said to him, "Teacher, what shall we do?"

And he said to them, "Collect no more than is appointed you."

Soldiers also asked him, "And we, what shall we do?"

And he said to them, "Rob no one by violence or by false accusation, and be content with your wages."

As the people were in expectation, and all men questioned in their hearts concerning John, whether perhaps he were the Christ, John answered them all, "I baptize you with water; but he who is mightier than I is coming, the thong of whose sandals I am not worthy to untie; he will baptize you with the Holy Spirit and with fire. His winnowing fork is in his hand, to clear his threshing floor, and to gather the wheat into his granary, but the chaff he will burn with unquenchable fire."

So, with many other exhortations, he preached good news to the people.

It's always worthwhile to gather as many facts as we can about these biblical characters, before we try to understand them as people.

Just as Jesus' birth is presented to us in Luke's gospel as a miraculous one, so John's birth is presented to us as remarkable, too. John was born, according to Luke, to an unlikely couple – to an older couple with no children, just as Isaac was born to Abraham and Sarah.

John was born as part of the fulfillment of God's plan, in accordance with a prophecy. Even before he was born, the angel Gabriel said John would be great.

We don't have a lot of hard information about John as he began his ministry. He appeared out of the wilderness, living a pure, ascetic life, dressed in the simplest of clothing.

I always like to stretch my imagination. I wonder what the people in these Bible stories *looked* like, or what they *sounded* like. I like to try different appearances on for size, and imagine different tones of voice than the ones I'm used to hearing.

We have a common mental picture of John as a wild-eyed religious maniac, eating locusts and wild honey and wearing itchy underwear. It's an easy caricature – the unkempt beard, the fanatic gleam in his eyes, the finger pointing up towards heaven.

Just for a change, I tried picturing John the Baptist as someone more approachable, as someone gentler and humbler than I usually imagine him. I tried picturing John as someone more like Francis of Assisi – a holy person, certainly, but a gentle extremist, somebody filled with the Holy Spirit, a beggar for God.

I don't know if that picture is accurate or not, but maybe it can help us as we try to hear John speaking, as we listen for the passion behind his message.

Most of the time, we think John must have been a pulpit-thumping preacher. You know, the sort of person who goes around laying guilt trips on people. *"You SINNERS! REPENT!"*

But the word "repent" literally means, "to turn one's heart or mind or life in a different direction." Repentance – ***metanoia*** in Greek – means *turning around.*

So instead of shouting at the top of his voice, maybe John was gently saying, "Turn around. Recognize what you're doing. Look at where you are. The way that you are taking is a way of death, a dead end. Look at where you're heading, and turn back. Turn the other way . . ."

I don't know which portrait you find more appealing – the wild-eyed fanatic or St. Francis. Maybe neither picture of John is truly accurate. But listening to his message in different tones of voice helps me to imagine what he could have been like.

John gathered his own circle of disciples and friends around him, just as Jesus would do later. One reason I'm inclined to see John in a gentler mode than we usually imagine him, is that according to the record, John was an *attractive* person. People were *drawn* to him. He had friends. People listened to him. People cared about him. In spite of the very pointed content of his message, people *loved* John.

Another reason to think about John in this new way, is that according to the record, John was able to *let go* later on. When Jesus began to preach, John told his friends, "It's OK. Follow him, not me. He must increase; I must decrease. That's why I came, to get people ready for him. He's the one . . ."

It's a measure of the greatness of John that he could say something like that, that he could recognize his own role as a servant, and rejoice in it. It takes a great personality to do such a thing – not a wild-eyed fanatic, not some half-crazed prophet from the desert. To understand who God is, and what God is doing, and gladly to accept second place – that takes gentleness, and humility.

Next, I'd like to look for a minute at the *content* of John's message – not just at *who* he was, but at *what* he said. And again, we don't have too many details.

For Jesus, we have whole books – entire gospels devoted to his life and teaching. For John, we have only a sketch, only an outline. The few definite things we know about John's teaching include:

1) a *radical social criticism*, which is something most of the Old Testament prophets included with their messages. John said that there was something wrong with the world, that there was a sickness in society. I don't know if he raised his voice when he said it, or not. But people listened.

2) John said that it was *people* who were at fault. John criticized rulers like Herod, and he attacked hypocrisy in all of its forms. "Don't think, because of who your ancestors were, that God approves of who you are, or what you do. It is your lives, and what you do, that matters. Those are the things that God sees. God can raise up a new people from the rocks and stones around you, if you let God down. . ."

3) John talked a lot about *baptism* – after all, that's why they called him "John the Baptist," wasn't it? He kept dunking people in water. It's not clear whether he just gave them a one-time slosh or whether they underwent repeated baptism, which was a common custom among Jews at the time. Some of the other religious groups like the Essenes practiced frequent baptism. But John talked about baptism as a sign of *change* in people's lives.

If you asked John which was the cart and which was the horse, or which was the chicken and which was the egg, John would say, "Clean up your life FIRST! Then come back and see me. This baptism that I give is a sign that you have turned around, that you have changed your life, that living in God's way really means something to you . . ."

If you want to be technical about it, changing your life is the *prior condition* of receiving baptism, from John's point of view. Baptism does not wash away sin; it is a sign that sin has *already* been turned away from and rooted out.

Part of the reason I feel it's worth taking a fresh look at John, is that it says that John's message came as *good news* to people. We usually picture John as a hellfire-and-damnation preacher, but Luke says that he brought *good news* to people. They were excited about it! They rejoiced over it. I don't think that most people act that way when they're being scolded.

The people who came to John asked him what to do. They called him "teacher" – Rabbi – the same word they later used to address Jesus. And they asked him, "What should we do?"

And John answered, "Let whoever has two coats, share with the person who has none. And let everyone who has food, do the same thing . . ."

Those aren't the words of a wild-eyed fanatic. Those words sound a lot to me like the teaching of Jesus – and they sound like the picture of the early Christian community in the book of Acts.

Other people who came to John had major lifestyle problems – people like tax collectors, and soldiers, and so on. John gave them very specific instructions about what changes they needed to make. "Give up extortion," he said. "Give up violence. Give up accusing people of things they haven't done. Do what you are appointed to do. Be content with what you have . . ."

And again, he said: "The baptism of the one who is coming after me is nothing like the baptism that I give. The sign that you have turned your lives around now is water; the sign that he will give is the Holy Spirit itself, and fire . . ."

That "fire" business always makes us nervous. We always think about hell fire, which maybe says something about our own bad conscience.

I'm not sure just what kind of fire John meant. Maybe it was the flame of Pentecost, when the Holy Spirit descended on the disciples. Or maybe it's the fire of trials and temptations, the fire of witness and martyrdom. You can wrestle with that one, and see where you come out with it.

The thing which is clear, as I read about John the Baptist, is that he meant to create a people who were *prepared for God.* He wanted people to be ready for what God was trying to do. He wanted to create a climate of expectation and excitement.

He wanted to see people actively preparing their lives, turning their lives around, so that when Jesus came along, people would already be headed in the right direction.

I'd like us to ask ourselves what being a prepared people could really mean. The whole point of John's message was, "Prepare ye the way of the Lord . . ."

What would that mean, for us? What would that be like? What would we be doing? What would be different?

Are we ready for something to happen, whenever we come to worship? Have our actions during the week prepared us? Is there anything we can point to and say, "This is what I did to get ready to bring myself before God this morning?"

And, of course, the question goes deeper than that. Because John didn't just want a group of well-dressed people to turn up at a special time for worship. John's whole point was that our *entire lives* need to be focused on preparation and on turning around.

Repentance needs to be absolutely *characteristic* of people who want to listen to John, and who want to follow in the footsteps of Christ. Not "repentance" meaning, "feeling guilty." Repentance is a lifelong habit or pursuit, a lifetime project of continually turning around or turning back, whenever we recognize we have gone the wrong way.

John calls us to make pathways straight; to bridge and level impassable valleys; to knock down and level mountains; to untangle the twisted and crooked places in our all-too-human lives. Maybe we won't get all the roughness out of our lives, but at least smooth it some. John calls us to work and prepare so that people around us can see what God is doing in the world.

II

What Does an Angel Look Like?

One year, as I got ready for Christmas, I found myself asking an unusual question. Maybe a foolish one. I started asking, "You know, what does an angel really *look like*?"

I'm sure that if I asked you, you would have one of two answers. Either you'd say:

1) "Well, I don't know. I've never seen one," or else you'd say,

2) "Well, *everybody* knows that! Angels wears long white robes and have wings and a halo."

The Bible doesn't really say what angels look like. You'd think that they might have given at least some details. But it doesn't say.

When artists try to represent angels, the standard picture is of a *human-like figure* with a robe and wings. I'm not sure why that is. Maybe the idea is to show that we're *close to* or *related to* the angels. In Psalm 8:5, it says that we human beings were created "a little lower than the angels." Maybe that's why artists make angels look human.

Maybe giving angels wings is meant to suggest the idea that angels are more *free* than we are – that they are freer of the kind of human restraints and limitations that we have. Angels probably don't worry about how to make their living, or where their next meal is coming from. They certainly seem to be able to zip around from one place to the other pretty easily.

One of the other things that artists usually do when they make pictures of angels, is they portray them as filled with *light*. There always seems to be a special glow or radiance whenever an angel turns up. That idea, of course, comes from the idea that God is filled with light, or that God *is* light, and that the closer we get to God, the brighter and clearer everything becomes.

Of course, other people will say that angels are really *invisible*. That's because their real job is to let God shine through them. So we don't see them, most of the time.

Angels are supposed to be very *beautiful*, and angels are also somewhat *terrifying*. At least, that's the way it always seems in the Bible. There is something which is both attractive and scary about angels. Maybe they're so completely different and amazing that ordinary people are scared of them. That almost seems like a paradox, to have something be both beautiful and terrifying at the same time.

But of course, there are more ways of understanding or picturing an angel, than as someone in a white robe with wings and a harp.

C.S. Lewis, one of the great Christian writers of the 20th century, wrote a series of books in which he pictured angels as bodiless, weightless and invisible – but totally alive! The angels Lewis wrote about aren't so much invisible, they just move at a *different speed* than we do. The things we do are at such a different speed that angels can barely notice us; the things that angels are involved with are done at such a different speed that we can barely imagine them.

Lewis' vision of the universe is very different from the one we tend to have. We think of outer space as being empty and cold. It's infinite, terrifying and threatening. Lewis shows space, from the angels' point of view, as being filled with *light*, as giving infinite *freedom*, and being filled with *movement* and *music*. The stars and planets are all a part of a great dance and a great song which goes on forever.

Another Christian writer, Madeleine L'Engle, suggests an entirely different vision of angels. The angels in Madeleine L'Engle's books are more like something you'd find in the Old Testament in the books of Daniel or Ezekiel.

Madeleine L'Engle's vision of what an angel looks like is something made up almost entirely of *wings* and *eyes*. The wings, of course, suggest movement, the ability to go anywhere and be anywhere, and the wings of her angels are constantly in motion. The many eyes, of course, suggest vision, and the ability to see into anything in the universe.

There's a marvelous part in Madeleine L'Engle's book, *A Wind in the Door*, where she talks about being caught up into the heart of one of these angelic creatures. She says that it's a wild, passionate, timeless, ageless, kind of feeling in an angel's heart – it's filled with flame and life.

There's another section where she says that the angels are always singing, all the time, which is another common idea about angels. But she says that the angels only know one song, and that song is: "Glory, glory, glory . . .!"

Well, I didn't mean to get off onto such a long digression about angels. But there's a lot of confusion about what they are and what they're supposed to look like.

During the Middle Ages, people got into all sorts of absurd discussions about this. One group of scholars is supposed to have seriously debated on how many angels could dance on the head of a pin.

You know, I've heard people say that all my life, and I've never come across the original source of that story. It's got to exist somewhere. Everyone's heard of it, but I've never found anyone who could show me where that story came from.

Anyway. All this is kind of a prelude or introduction, because we're about to meet an angel. And I thought it might sharpen your curiosity if you started wondering what an angel would look like, or sound like, before we meet the angel in the story. As you read along, try to imagine yourself in the story, as if the angel were speaking to you, or as if you were the angel.

Luke 1:5-38

In the days of Herod, king of Judea, there was a priest named Zechariah, of the division of Abijah; and he had a wife of the daughters of Aaron, and her name was Elizabeth. And they were both righteous before God, walking in all the commandments and ordinances of the Lord blameless. But they had no child, because Elizabeth was barren, and both were advanced in years.

Now while he was serving as priest before God when his division was on duty, according to the custom of the priesthood, it fell to him by lot to enter the temple of the Lord and burn incense. And the whole multitude of the people were praying outside at the hour of incense. And there appeared to him an angel of the Lord standing on the right side of the altar of incense. And Zechariah was troubled when he saw him, and fear fell upon him.

But the angel said to him, "Do not be afraid, Zechariah, for your prayer is heard, and your wife Elizabeth will bear you a son, and you shall call his name John. And you will have joy and gladness, and many will rejoice at his birth; for he will be great before the Lord, and he shall drink no wine nor strong drink, and he will be filled with the Holy Spirit, even from his mother's womb. And he will turn many of the sons of Israel to the Lord their God, and he will go before him in the spirit and power of Elijah, to turn the hearts of the fathers to the children, and the disobedient to the wisdom of the just, to make ready for the Lord a people prepared."

And Zechariah said to the angel, "How shall I know this? For I am an old man, and my wife is advanced in years."

And the angel answered him, "I am Gabriel, who stand in the presence of God; and I was sent to speak to you, and to bring you this good news. And behold, you will be silent and unable to speak until the day that these things come to pass, because you did not believe my words, which will be fulfilled in their time."

And the people were waiting for Zechariah, and they wondered at his delay in the And when he came out, he could not speak to them, and they perceived that he had seen a vision in the temple; and he made signs to them and remained dumb. And when his time of service was ended, he went to his home.

After these days his wife Elizabeth conceived, and for five months she hid herself, saying, "Thus the Lord has done to me in the days when he looked on me, to take away my reproach among men."

In the sixth month the angel Gabriel was sent from God to a city of Galilee named Nazareth, to a virgin betrothed to a man whose name was Joseph, of the house of David; and the virgin's name was Mary. And he came to her and said, "Hail, O favored one, the Lord is with you!"

But she was greatly troubled at the saying, and considered in her mind what sort of greeting this might be.

And the angel said to her, "Do not be afraid, Mary, for you have found favor with God. And behold, you will conceive in your womb and bear a son, and you shall call his name Jesus. He will be great, and will be called the Son of the Most High; and the Lord God will give to him the throne of his father David, and he will reign over the house of Jacob for ever; and of his kingdom there will be no end."

And Mary said to the angel, "How shall this be, since I have no husband?"

And the angel said to her, "The Holy Spirit will come upon you, and the power of the Most High will overshadow you; therefore the child to be born will be called holy, the Son of God. And behold, your kinswoman Elizabeth in her old age has also conceived a son; and this is the sixth month with her who was called barren. For with God nothing will be impossible."

And Mary said, "Behold, I am the handmaid of the Lord; let it be to me according to your word."

And the angel departed from her.

You can do a lot of things with that story.

You can believe it, or you can disbelieve it. You can ask a lot of silly questions about it, like: "Well, what did the angel *really* look like?" or, "Was Mary *really* a virgin?" or, "Isn't this whole business kind of strange and unlikely?"

And I'm not going to try to answer any of those questions. I think that belief, or disbelief, is up to every one of us. You can treat it as fact, or fiction, whichever way your mind and your heart tell you.

I don't insist that people believe in angels. I don't know that I've ever seen an angel, myself. The Bible only talks about them a little bit. In some ways, it would make the world less complicated if there was just the world, and God, and us, without cluttering things up by adding lots of angels or invisible beings all over the place.

But either way, if angels *don't* exist, then I don't think that just believing in them will make them exist. And if angels *do* exist, and we don't believe in them, then I think that God is somehow big enough to be able to handle our disbelief. I don't know. Maybe God'll send me an angel some day, and maybe I'll be in shape to notice.

What I'd like to focus on, instead, is the *content* of the messages which Gabriel brought in this gospel reading.

The first message was to Zacharias, the priest who Gabriel met in the Temple. And, you know, you almost get the feeling that Zacharias himself didn't believe in angels, before all this happened.

Even though he was a priest, even though he had inherited the position, even though he believed in God, even though he *knew* that marvelous things are supposed to happen, you almost get the feeling that Zacharias himself didn't believe.

He thought that prayer was important, and he thought that worship was important. Being selected to go in and burn the incense in the Temple was a really special honor. It was a once-in-a-lifetime privilege for him. It was a whole lot more important than being sent out to the playground to pound the chalk dust out of the erasers, or whatever routine jobs priests had then.

But you don't get the feeling that Zacharias actually *expected* anything to happen that day, when he went in to do his priestly duty. Maybe he felt honored, maybe he felt excited, maybe he felt holy – but he sure didn't expect to see an angel!

He never expected whatever it was that he saw – whether it was a humanlike figure with a robe and wings, glowing with light, or a fantastic creature like Madeleine L'Engle's being of eyes and wings and passion and fire, or something else we can't even imagine. Whatever it was that Zacharias saw, it wasn't anything he expected.

And then the angel said, "Don't let me scare you!"

Well, of course he was scared. He must have been terrified! I don't know if angels are beautiful or scary to look at. Maybe both. But the utterly unexpected is always scary.

And then the angel said that Zacharias and his wife Elizabeth would have a son, a child who they would name

John, who would grow up and become the person we know as John the Baptist. I won't go into all of the details of the prophecy, but it's clear that this child was going to be somebody special.

When I've looked at this passage before, I've always been impressed by something in Gabriel's message. The angel said: "I am Gabriel, who stand in the presence of the Lord . . ."

There's an ambiguity about that line for me; you can take it a couple of ways. It could mean that Gabriel was a *senior* or *special* angel, one who had the right or privilege of standing before God, instead of kneeling or whatever.

Or it could mean that Gabriel, as an angel, could be many places at once. That is, Gabriel could be right there, talking to Zacharias, and at the same time Gabriel could *also* be somewhere else, standing in the very presence of God, right in that same moment. I always find that ambiguity intriguing.

Now let's look at another part of Gabriel's message. The standard translation of what Gabriel prophesied about John is: " . . .He will turn the hearts of fathers to their children. . ." That makes it sound as if John's mission in life was going to be *reconciling families*, which is certainly a good thing to do.

But another translation says: "He will soften adult hearts to become like little children's, and he will change disobedient minds to the wisdom of faith. . ."

In a way, that sounds more like what John really did. And it kind of fits in with what Jesus said, about "Unless you become like a little child, you shall never enter the kingdom . . ." (Matthew 18:3)

Anyway, Gabriel said that Zacharias and Elizabeth were going to have a son, even though they were both just about ready to collect Social Security. And Gabriel didn't talk about this as a *possibility*, or even as something that would happen in the future. Gabriel stated it as if it were already an accomplished *fact*. That's what a prophecy is.

And Zacharias' response wasn't simply to say Yes or No. He didn't just accept or reject what the angel said. Instead, he questioned whether God could do it at all.

And it was because of that, that Zacharias was struck dumb until the baby was actually born. I don't know if it was a punishment. Maybe it was simply a case of, "Because you did not answer today, you will have nothing to say, until you see it happen."

A little while later, the angel Gabriel was sent to a young woman, to Mary, the cousin of Zacharias' wife Elizabeth. Maybe the angel had learned not to present such a frightening appearance, or maybe Gabriel was trying to calm her down, because the first thing Gabriel said this time was, "Peace be with you!"

I know that in the old King James version, it says, "Hail!" But I looked it up in the original, and what it really says is, "Peace be with you!" If Mary spoke either Hebrew or Aramaic, what the angel would have said to her was,

"***Shalom*** . . . !" That is the greeting of the angel to Mary. *Peace* is the first word of the Annunciation.

And of course Mary, like Zacharias, was confused and scared. So would you or I be, if an angel appeared unexpectedly to us.

And so the angel said, "Don't be afraid, Mary; God loves you very much . . ." The first word is *peace*; the second word is *love*. God called to her by name, and God told her that she didn't have to be afraid. That's part of the message of Advent and Christmas, too – "Don't be afraid, God loves you very much . . ."

And then Gabriel went on to tell her, in much the same way that the angel had earlier spoken to Zacharias, that because of God, there would be a child, a child who by ordinary expectations would never have even been born.

And then the angel explained, in a way that's probably as clear as we are ever going to be able to understand, how the whole thing was going to take place.

And then the angel *waited*. Gabriel, the messenger of God, the one who stood in the very presence of God, had to wait on the answer of a scared, confused young woman. In many famous paintings that I've seen of this event, there's the feeling that the whole world is waiting on the answer that Mary will give. The whole world can go one way, or another, depending on what she says next.

And where Zacharias had doubted, where Zacharias had questioned God's ability to do what Gabriel foretold, Mary's response was different. Mary *accepted*. She said, "I am the

Lord's servant, and I am willing to do whatever the Lord wants. May everything you have said come true."

And after that the angel went away, in whatever way that angels go. Maybe they flutter out the window. Maybe they just disappear, or fade away. If an angel is someone who has one foot in this world and one foot in heaven, maybe the angel just stepped back. It doesn't say.

But what's clear is that Mary's answer was the one that God needed. God needed Mary to say *Yes*.

It's as though every time God says something, or does something, there's a blank space, or an empty line at the end. Every time we read one of these stories about God coming into the world, there's a *response* needed. It's as though every story in the Bible has written at the end of it, "R.S.V.P."

I don't know how God would announce the birth of Christ in the world today, if God were to do it all over again. Maybe the story would be just the same – maybe Mary would be someone we know and recognize, from our own neighborhood. Or maybe she would be from some Third World country, or speak a different language than Hebrew, or be of a different race.

I think that the greeting God sends is timeless. God says, "Peace be with you, you to whom special grace has been given; the Lord is with you."

That message is for all of us. It doesn't just come to Mary, it comes to every one of us. The peace of knowing that God is there, the peace of Christ, the peace that is meant for the whole world, is offered to us.

And then, just as it was for Mary, the message for us is: "Do not be afraid; God loves you very dearly . . ."

The gift that Christ brings is not only peace, but freedom from fear, and the assurance of God's love.

And whenever God speaks, just as with Mary, there are always *promises*. Maybe not the birth of a son, for us, but certainly the birth of a Savior. That promise is always there for us, too.

And then, God waits. Messages from God always end, "R.S.V.P." Respond, if you please. Please answer. Not just during Advent, not just at Christmas, but always. God gives us a Savior, and then God *waits* – to see what our answer will be.

III

Led By a Little Child

You can tell it's Advent. We're surrounded with advertisements and TV specials and community events. All of them are telling us that "it's time to get ready for Christmas."

I agree. It *is* time for us to be getting ready for Christmas. But not necessarily in the way that everybody says we're supposed to be getting ready.

I think it's nice to have fun in the month of December. But I don't think we necessarily have to buy in to all of the things people say about Christmas every year. And I don't just mean the commercialism that everybody complains about. I get tired of all the canned Christmas music in the stores, just like you. I get tired of all the hype. And I think that it's silly that children aren't allowed to sing Christmas carols in school any more, not even "Silent Night."

But those complaints are all on the surface. I think we've got some deeper work to do before Christmas, some deeper digging into our attitudes and misconceptions.

For example, it's natural for us to picture the events of Christmas as taking place in our own kind of country, in our own sort of climate. For those of us who live in North

America, we naturally tend to think that Christmas means snowflakes falling, and evergreen trees all covered with sparkling frost, and things like that. That's because we live in a part of the world where it's usually pretty cold around December 25th.

Since most of Northern Europe shares something of the same climate, we've got a lot of songs and pictures and mental images all focused around having a "white Christmas."

In Australia, December is the hottest part of the summer. I imagine it's hard to sing, "Deck the Halls With Boughs of Holly," or "Frosty the Snowman," when it's 110° in the shade down in Queensland. I remember reading about a teacher in Australia who was trying to explain to the children about snow. She had a lot of difficulty, because she'd never even seen the stuff herself.

But that's just one example of the kind of narrow-mindedness and insularity that we tend to have about Christmas. It's a challenge for us to try to imagine what Christmas must mean to people in other parts of the world, who see Christmas through their own eyes and experience.

What do you suppose Christmas feels like to someone in Brazil, for example, or over in Africa? Or what does the coming of the Christ Child mean to somebody in India, or Indonesia? What does Christmas mean when you can't afford a pile of presents, if you've got to be grateful just for your next meal?

Putting the focus of Christmas on the weather, or snow, or Santa Claus, is really pretty misleading. It has to be about something deeper than that.

I think that we also need to be careful in our unconscious expectations about how Jesus and his family looked. The majority of people in the U.S. are white, and so are the majority of people in Western Europe. Most of our pictures of the Nativity naturally portray Jesus as a white baby. In a lot of old Sunday School pictures, Jesus used to have blond hair and blue eyes.

But what does Jesus look like to other people around the world? What if Jesus wasn't a white baby after all? What if Jesus' skin was a little bit darker than ours? Or what if Mary had a hooked nose?

In my library I have a copy of Roland Bainton's wonderful book, "Behold the Christ." It's filled with pictures of how people in other countries have portrayed the life of Jesus. The first time I looked through it, I saw pictures of an African Joseph holding a black baby Jesus, and Korean wise men visiting the stable. You see, people who come to Christ understand that Jesus really *looks like them*, because Christ came to *be one of us*.

So there's a picture of an American Indian Nativity, with the parents wearing feathers and paint. And there's a 13th-century medieval French carving of the massacre of the innocents, which shows Herod's soldiers all wearing armor and chain mail.

One of my favorites is a picture of Mary and Joseph being turned away from a Chinese inn. It's painted on silk, and it shows the inn surrounded by a bamboo fence, with a water buffalo in the background.

What if Jesus *didn't* look just like us? Or what if we have to join the rest of the people of the world, in trying to imagine what he looked like? What if we don't "own" Jesus?

It isn't just that we need to "share" Jesus generously with the rest of the world. What if we have to change our understanding, and realize that it was God who shared Christ with us, and that we have to take our place in sharing him along with everybody else?

That's only one example of the kind of re-thinking that I think we need to do. We don't own Jesus, and we don't own Christmas. We receive Jesus, as a *gift*. Jesus is God's gift to the entire world, and we need to understand that deep down in our minds and hearts.

And while we're at it, we might as well come out into the open and say that there wasn't a tree there that first Christmas. There weren't any carols, no matter how much we enjoy them. There wasn't a Little Drummer Boy, at least not outside of legend. In fact, we could probably strip away about 99% of the stuff we've attached to Christmas, if we wanted to try to get to the real story of what happened.

I'd like look with you now at a reading from the Old Testament, from one of the prophecies of Isaiah about the coming of Christ.

Isaiah 11:1-9

There shall come forth a shoot from the stump of Jesse, and a branch shall grow out of his roots.

And the Spirit of the LORD shall rest upon him, the spirit of wisdom and understanding, the spirit of counsel and might, the spirit of knowledge and the fear of the LORD. And his delight shall be in the fear of the LORD.

He shall not judge by what his eyes see, or decide by what his ears hear; but with righteousness he shall judge the poor, and decide with equity for the meek of the earth; and he shall smite the earth with the rod of his mouth, and with the breath of his lips he shall slay the wicked. Righteousness shall be the girdle of his waist, and faithfulness the girdle of his loins.

The wolf shall dwell with the lamb, and the leopard shall lie down with the kid, and the calf and the lion and the fatling together, and a little child shall lead them.

The cow and the bear shall feed; their young shall lie down together; and the lion shall eat straw like the ox. The sucking child shall play over the hole of the serpent, and the weaned child shall put his hand on the serpent's den. They shall not hurt or destroy in all my holy mountain; for the earth shall be full of the knowledge of the LORD as the waters cover the sea.

That was what people knew about, when Jesus was born into the world. That prophecy was all they had to go on. It represented nearly everything that they knew about the coming of Christ.

And people had had plenty of time to think about it, while they were waiting. Isaiah's message had been delivered 700 years before Jesus was born. People had been trying to figure out what to expect from God for at least that long.

Imagine what we would do, or what we would think, if we'd been waiting around for 700 years for God to do something. What would our expectations be? How many people today, do you suppose, would be willing to change their lives based on a promise given 200 years before Columbus? Or how many of us would be able to build their understanding of the world on a message given 500 years before the American Revolution?

I bring that up, because it's easy for us to think to ourselves how short-sighted the people of Jesus' day were, how unready they were to accept the idea that this baby born in a manger, this person from a back-water town in Galilee, this unknown son of an unknown carpenter, was the Savior God had promised.

I'm not sure that we would be ready to believe it, either. I'm not sure that we believe it, even now.

I think that, just like the people of Jesus' day, we are much too quick to expect Christ to be someone powerful and glorious. And we're much too slow to think about the message that Isaiah really delivered.

It starts off with a verse that's almost in code. It says, "There shall come forth a shoot from the stump of Jesse . . ." Now, we've all heard the Christmas story before, and everybody knows that means that the Messiah was going to be a descendant of King David. Jesse was David's father. Therefore, the promised king was going to be one of his descendants.

But there's a little more to it than that. It says from the *stump* of Jesse, and it says "a branch (or a twig) will grow out of his roots . . ." You have to realize how nearly destroyed Israel was at that time. Jesus was born in a country which had been occupied by invaders for generations. Whole sections of the population had been deported, or had fled into exile. Several layers of alien culture had been imposed onto the country. They had been oppressed and dispossessed for hundreds of years. If you want a parallel, you would have to say that Jesus was born into a country very much like El Salvador, or Guatemala, or South Africa, or one of the Balkan states.

It's out of a place like that, said Isaiah, that the Messiah will come. He won't be from one of the best and the brightest families. Nor from the rich and the privileged. God's son would be born from a poor nation, Isaiah said, from one which had gone back to its roots, because everything else had been destroyed.

"And the Spirit of the Lord shall rest upon him, the spirit of wisdom and understanding, the spirit of counsel and might, the spirit of knowledge and the fear of the Lord, and his delight shall be in the fear of the Lord . . ." That part is relatively easy for us to understand. It's more nearly the sort of thing we would expect from somebody who God had sent to us.

One quick comment: a lot of people today are uncomfortable with the phrase "the fear of the Lord." Most of us think that Jesus came to teach us *not* to be afraid of God. After all, didn't Jesus teach us that God is love? What place does fear have in our understanding?

That phrase, "the fear of the Lord," is one you run across a lot in the Old Testament. And it doesn't mean carrying around a lot of guilt or remorse, or being scared all the time that God is going to zap you. Rather, it means a sort of a healthy religious respect, a kind of an awe or reverence that affects everything you do.

To talk about "the fear of the Lord" means that we recognize that God is *alive*, that God is a living force in our world. It means that no matter where we go or what we do, God has to be reckoned with.

Yes, in a way, it means fear. It means, "Aren't you *afraid* to do those kinds of things, things that you *know* are wrong? Don't you know that God really exists?"

There are a lot of people around today who you wish would ask themselves those questions. Politicians, and lawyers, and generals, and business people, and families, and individuals – you wish that they would ask themselves things like that. "How can you *do* those things? Don't you ever consider what *God* thinks about what you're doing? Don't you ever wonder how what you do will be judged – not by public opinion polls or by the numbers in your bank account, but by God?"

That's what "fearing God" means. But it also means something deeper. Once you get past the level of simply being afraid, once you enter into a relationship with God, you get to the place where it becomes important to *maintain* that relationship. That's what Isaiah meant when he prophesied that the Messiah's *delight* would be in "the fear of the Lord."

If you look at Jesus, that's exactly the kind of person he was. Jesus wasn't afraid. But Jesus also knew how much God mattered. Jesus wasn't crippled by his understanding of God. He wasn't neurotic. He didn't go around afraid to talk to people, or to afraid eat with them, or afraid to be seen with them, because it might make him "less holy."

Jesus was only afraid that he might not *listen to God*. And because he spent so much time in intimate contact with God, because his life was so completely filled with the Holy Spirit, even that fear didn't bother Jesus all that much.

Then there's the section where Isaiah talks about *judgment*. It says, "He shall not judge by what his eyes see, or decide by what his ears hear; but with righteousness he shall judge the poor, and decide with equity for the meek of the earth . . ."

Again, that's pretty straightforward. Christ isn't interested in what people say, in their public image, or in gossip of any kind. Christ isn't interested in appearances, but in reality. And Christ is interested in people who are hungry and thirsty for things to be right.

It also says – and we all know it, but it hasn't really sunk in to us – that God is really more interested in the *poor*, than in people who are already well-off. God always decides on behalf of the *humble*, on behalf of people who are unable to speak up for themselves.

God's real interest is always in people who aren't able to make ends meet, in people who are confused and intimidated by all of the government forms and paperwork that they need to fill out in order to get the basic necessities of food and clothing and help that they need.

God cares about people who can never break out of poverty, and God judges the people who keep them there. God cares deeply for all of the people who aren't as bright, who can't think as well or as clearly, who don't have the advantages, who were simply born into places where they can't live decently.

God is on their side. And if we're not actively on their side, then we are not on God's side. That's what Isaiah is saying. If you don't like it, don't argue with me. Go argue with God.

Then we get to the part that originally attracted me to this passage, the part that everybody knows by heart, and which we don't really think very deeply about. "The wolf shall dwell with the lamb, and the leopard shall lie down with the kid, and the calf and the lion and the fat sheep shall be together, and a little child shall lead them. . ." That's such a beautiful picture, and we let go of it much too quickly.

When I got started on this passage, I decided that I was going to hang onto that image of the Peaceable Kingdom until I understood it better. And so every day, I asked myself, "What does it mean when it says, `A little child shall lead them'?"

We often read this passage at Christmas, because we like to think of the little child, the baby in the manger. And we think about the animals gathered in the stable, and everything calm and quiet and peaceful.

And that's OK. Even if we didn't push it any farther than that, what does it mean to be *led* by the newborn baby Jesus?

Christmas doesn't mean gifts, and advertising, and Muzak at the malls, and all the other things we spend so much of our time and energy on. If we forget all that stuff, Christmas hasn't lost anything. But if we forget the newborn Christ, then Christmas is meaningless.

Christmas means letting our lives be led by God's Son, helpless and in need of our total care. Christmas means facing up to all of the grubby details of making a home in a stable.

Christmas also means thinking about what Jesus said: "Unless you become like a little child, you shall never enter the Kingdom of Heaven. . ."

Christmas means accepting the gift of a child-like approach to the truth, and making that gift a distinctive part of our lives. It means taking on the humility of a child, and the total trust of a child.

It means welcoming joy, and it means wanting peace. No child in this world who has ever seen the real face of war up close, ever wants to have anything to do with war again.

That picture of the lion and the lamb living together in Isaiah is so fantastic, that we either sentimentalize it, or else we dismiss it without trying to take it seriously. Everybody knows that it's going against nature for that sort of thing to happen. And God says, "*Exactly.* That's exactly right." God is talking about a change in nature, a change that enables warring parties and ancient enemies to make peace with one another.

If Christmas is about anything, Christmas is about *peace*. It's about accepting the gift of a permanent and total change in our hearts and in our lives, a change away from the nature that we're so used to, a change into the kind of people that God wants us so much to be.

Christ invites us to give up our old and terribly human nature, and to accept a new nature, given to us by God. That's a gift that keeps on giving. We are invited to accept the gift of Christ into our lives. And we're invited to let that baby Jesus grow up into full maturity in our lives as well.

Isaiah presents us with a vision of a world which is filled with the knowledge of God. Instead of little stories and little glimpses, like the ones we get at Christmas, we are invited to a vision of a whole world which knows God and loves God.

The gift which we are offered is nothing less than a new world, one which isn't led by politicians and generals and bankers and pressure groups, but one which is led in peace by a little child.

IV

The Gift of Christmas

Christmas is a lot of fun, but at times it seems as though there's been *too much* of everything. Too much build-up, too many celebrations, too many special events, all in too little time. A lot of people I talk with feel that they're under the stress of too many obligations. It's supposed to be a joyful time, but for too many people it's a stressful time, or a lonely time, or a difficult time.

And I suppose we sometimes contribute to all of those extra problems that crop up and crowd us around Christmas. Maybe we load too much on ourselves. We all want to have fun, but maybe it ought to be simpler.

I thought I'd start out this meditation by talking about the right way to open presents. You see, there's a right way, and a wrong way to approach our gifts. The wrong way is to tear through them, to open them all as quickly as possible, to rip open one toy and demand to be given the next. And then, when you're all finished, you get cranky, and you sit and veg out in front of the TV for the rest of the day.

That's one wrong way to open your presents. Another wrong way is to concentrate on all of the unimportant things, like disposing of the wrapping paper instead of enjoying the moment, or getting everybody lined up for the pictures, or making sure that all of the names get taken down neatly for the thank-you notes. If you do that, you miss a lot of the fun.

The right way, as I'm sure everybody knows, but as we so often forget, is to take our time. The right way to open presents is to open them slowly.

In our family, we only open one gift at a time. Each person gets to take a turn opening a gift. After it's opened, they get a minute to enjoy it, and try it, and handle it. Then, each gift gets passed around, so that everyone has a chance to look at it for themselves.

The youngest ones take turns passing out the gifts, so that they get to share in the pleasure of giving them. Every gift is handed out by a little child.

And as we open the gifts, we talk about other Christmases, so that there's a link made between the joys we've had in the past, and the joy we're having now, and the joys we'll have one day in the future. Nobody watches the clock. There's no hurry about it. There's only joy.

And when the gifts are all opened, there's all the time in the world to play with them, and take pleasure in them, and share them again. And it's like that, all day long.

That's the right way to open your presents. And maybe that does have something to do with what I want to say about

Christmas. I wish that we could slow down our pace just a little, and take time to enjoy it all more. Because I think it's supposed to be that way, all year.

And now, I'd like to slow down just a little, and recover that sense of what it's all supposed to be about, as we lay everything aside, and come together to the stable.

Luke 2:1-20 (KJV)

And it came to pass in those days, that there went out a decree from Caesar Augustus that all the world should be taxed. (And this taxing was first made when Cyrenius was governor of Syria.) And all went to be taxed, each to his own city.

And Joseph also went up from Galilee, out of the city of Nazareth, into Judea, unto the city of David, which is called Bethlehem; (because he was of the house and lineage of David), to be taxed with Mary, his espoused wife, being great with child.

And so it was that while they were there, the days were accomplished that she should be delivered. And she brought forth her first-born son and wrapped him in swaddling cloths, and laid him in a manger, because there was no room for them in the inn.

And there were in the same country shepherds abiding in the field, keeping watch over their flock by night. And lo, the angel of the Lord came upon them, and the glory of the Lord shone round about them: and they were sore afraid.

And the angel said unto them, "Fear not; for behold, I bring you tidings of great joy, which shall be to all people; for unto you is born this day in the city of David a Savior, who is Christ the Lord. And this will be a sign unto you: you shall find the babe wrapped in swaddling cloths and lying in a manger."

And suddenly there was with the angel a multitude of the heavenly host praising God and saying, "Glory to God in the highest, and on earth peace, good will toward men!"

And it came to pass, as the angels were gone away from them into heaven, the shepherds said one to another, "Let us now go even unto Bethlehem and see this thing which has come to pass, which the Lord has made known to us." And they came with haste, and found Mary and Joseph, and the babe lying in a manger.

And when they had seen it, they made known abroad the saying which was told them concerning this child; and all they that heard it wondered at those things which were told them by the shepherds. But Mary kept all these things, and pondered them in her heart. And the shepherds returned, glorifying and praising God for all the things that they had heard and seen, as it had been told unto them.

I suppose there is nothing new which could be said about that story. Every phrase of it is familiar to us. Many of us probably know it by heart, and could repeat it word for word if we wanted to.

And yet, like every good gift, it's always new. It doesn't matter whether we've received the same present before or not. The gift is always new. And we are there, seeing it all again, just as if this were Bethlehem, as if this room were the stable, just as if this were the hillside where the shepherds received the good news.

Christmas means many things. We've been talking about some of those things all through these meditations. It means things we don't think about.

Just for example: we don't usually think about the *context* of the Christmas story. It begins with an imperial decree going out from the emperor of Rome, the most powerful man in the world, the conqueror, the general. Caesar Augustus had conquered the known world of his day.

And through his conquests, he had brought peace. It was a peace that had to be maintained by occupying armies; it was a peace which had to be maintained through nearly unbearable taxes. Those taxes were the reason that Joseph and Mary had to go up to Bethlehem, the imperial taxes of Rome. But there was peace.

Caesar Augustus, like nearly all of the emperors, had himself proclaimed divine. Emperors like to do that. All through the Roman Empire, statues were put up of him, and on many of the statues were inscriptions which proclaimed

Caesar as the savior of the world. People worshiped Caesar then, as I suppose we still do in many places today.

But while the census was going on, at the very moment when the officials were counting just how many people were going to be paying their taxes to Almighty Caesar, something else was going on. In a small town, in the most obscure province of a corner of the Roman Empire, the true Savior of the world was being born.

Emperors are born in palaces; the Savior of the world was born in the stable of an overcrowded public inn. Right away, Christmas means *contrasts*. It means the arrival of the unexpected. Christmas always means a surprise.

There are so many things that we tend to forget about Christmas. We forget the jolting of the ride to Bethlehem for Mary, the ride on the back of a donkey or a camel. If I were a woman, if I'd ever been pregnant, I would probably have a much more vivid sense of how difficult that ride would have been for someone eight and a half or nine months along.

And we forget the weariness, the endless exhaustion and frustration of waiting to register at the tax office. If you have ever had to stand in line, or wait to deal with officialdom, you know what that felt like. The hours go by, and the lines don't move, and you just wait until it's your turn to be processed by someone who doesn't care, and who only wants to collect your money.

It may be a little harder for us to understand and sympathize with Joseph and Mary, as they tried to find a place to stay.

It's hard for us to feel the anger and the rejection in those simple lines, "there was no room for them in the inn. . ."

I imagine them going from place to place, going from shelter to shelter, only to be turned away at every door. I imagine Joseph crying aloud in the middle of the street, "This town is supposed to be my home! You say that I *belong* here! You *made* me come here! And now you say there isn't any place for me and for my wife and for my baby that's about to be born!"

Maybe if we really enter the Christmas story, we'd understand what homeless people feel like. Maybe we'd understand better what Jesus was talking about when he said, "Foxes have holes and birds of the air have nests, but the Son of Man has no place to lay his head . . ." (Matthew 8:20)

And then we come to the angels. We always have trouble believing in angels. They're not part of our practical, common-sense world.

I went out on an errand late one night this month. And as I walked outside, I happened to notice my shadow on the ground. It was ten or eleven o'clock at night, and there was my shadow, as clear as if it was day. I looked up and everything around me, was lit up just as clearly.

It was the moon, of course. We had a very full moon that week. But for just one moment, I could understand what it would be like to be caught in that completely unexpected glory in the middle of the night time.

On another night, one of those clear, cold nights we have in early winter, I went out and looked up at the stars. Millions of stars. And I remembered that one of the names of God in the Old Testament was **Yahweh Sabaoth,** "the Lord of hosts." When you look up at the sky, and look out into that infinite darkness and into that infinite blaze of light and glory, it's a little easier to believe that angels might be out there.

I found myself wondering how long the song of the angels went on for, that night when they sang. Because when you lift up your eyes, when you look up at the glory of God, then time stands still.

I know that it's completely speculative and irresponsible to be thinking about angels. Either they're there, or they're not. Most of the time, we sure don't see them. The world seems to be pretty quiet, if you go around listening for angels. Maybe God wants them to hold back and stay quiet most of the time.

But maybe just once, that night, all those angels lost their heads, and had to shout and sing. Maybe it was as simple as that. Maybe the rest of the time they have to hold back and keep quiet, but just this once they had to shake loose and shout.

And the reason was the good news that they had been given.

> *"Joy to the world! the Lord is come!*
> *Let earth receive her King!*
> *Let every heart prepare Him room,*
> *And heaven and nature sing! . . ."*

Maybe that's what it's all about. When the good news is joy to the world, when the good news is peace, when the good news is the birth of the one and only Savior, maybe you have to sing a little bit. Maybe you have to sing a lot. Maybe you have to do hand springs and cartwheels in heaven, and scare poor innocent shepherds silly, because it's all finally happening in a stable, in a manger.

Oh, yes. The shepherds. I almost forgot them.

We almost forget the shepherds – at least, we forget them the way they really were, and we forget what it really means for the birth of Christ to be announced to them. I said that the shepherds were poor. They were more than that, they were illiterate. They were considered untouchable. They were social outcasts, unclean.

The good news was given to people like that. It wasn't given to the power brokers and the crisis managers and the national security advisers. People like that can't receive it. They deal with a different sort of kingdom.

The good news was revealed to a handful of shepherds on a hillside, to simple people who could still understand and accept what they had been told by the angels.

Too many people can't understand that simple message: "Glory in heaven, and peace on earth . . .Glory in heaven, and peace on earth . . ."

And the angel didn't say that as some kind of a far-away promise. The angel said *today*. "For to you is born this day in the city of David a Savior, who is Christ the Lord. . ." *Today*.

Christmas means *today*. It means *now*. And that's all the more reason for joy. Glory in heaven, and peace on earth – today.

I wish you all a merry Christmas. But I also wish you all something more. I wish you all the birth of the Savior. I wish you joy, and peace. I wish you all the greatest gift there is: the Savior, who is Christ the Lord.

V

Joseph, the Dreamer

Every year, I try to find something different about the Christmas story. It always seems to me that there's something new.

Most of the time, when we read Matthew's version of the Christmas story, we talk about the three wise men. We might focus on the search for wisdom. Or we might talk about the difference between their kind of wisdom and the expedient, worldly wisdom of Herod.

Or we might talk about the gifts the wise men brought, and go blathering on and on about the symbolism of the gold, frankincense and myrrh.

Instead, I'd like to spend a few moments looking at a person who hardly appears at all outside the Christmas story; a person who comes into focus for just a little while, and then drops out of the picture again; Joseph, the carpenter, the patron saint of fathers everywhere, who is one of the least-known figures in the New Testament.

Matthew 1:18-2:23

Now the birth of Jesus Christ took place in this way.

When his mother Mary had been betrothed to Joseph, before they came together she was found to be with child of the Holy Spirit; and her husband Joseph, being a just man and unwilling to put her to shame, resolved to divorce her quietly.

But as he considered this, behold, an angel of the Lord appeared to him in a dream, saying, "Joseph, son of David, do not fear to take Mary your wife, for that which is conceived in her is of the Holy Spirit; she will bear a son, and you shall call his name Jesus, for he will save his people from their sins."

All this took place to fulfil what the Lord had spoken by the prophet: "Behold, a virgin shall conceive and bear a son, and his name shall be called Emmanuel" (which means, God with us). When Joseph woke from sleep, he did as the angel of the Lord commanded him; he took his wife, but knew her not until she had borne a son; and he called his name Jesus.

Now when Jesus was born in Bethlehem of Judea in the days of Herod the king, behold, wise men from the East came to Jerusalem, saying, "Where is he who has been born king of the Jews? For we have seen his star in the East, and have come to worship him."

When Herod the king heard this, he was troubled, and all Jerusalem with him; and assembling all the chief priests and scribes of the people, he inquired of them where the Christ was to be born.

They told him, "In Bethlehem of Judea; for so it is written by the prophet: 'And you, O Bethlehem, in the land of Judah, are by no means least among the rulers of Judah; for from you shall come a ruler who will govern my people Israel.'"

Then Herod summoned the wise men secretly and ascertained from them what time the star appeared; and he sent them to Bethlehem, saying, "Go and search diligently for the child, and when you have found him bring me word, that I too may come and worship him."

When they had heard the king they went their way; and lo, the star which they had seen in the East went before them, till it came to rest over the place where the child was. When they saw the star, they rejoiced exceedingly with great joy; and going into the house they saw the child with Mary his mother, and they fell down and worshiped him. Then, opening their treasures, they offered him gifts, gold and frankincense and myrrh. And being warned in a dream not to return to Herod, they departed to their own country by another way.

Now when they had departed, behold, an angel of the Lord appeared to Joseph in a dream and said, "Rise, take the child and his mother, and flee to Egypt, and remain there till I tell you; for Herod is about to search for the child, to destroy him."

And he rose and took the child and his mother by night, and departed to Egypt, and remained there until the death of Herod. This was to fulfil what the Lord had spoken by the prophet, "Out of Egypt have I called my son."

Then Herod, when he saw that he had been tricked by the wise men, was in a furious rage, and he sent and killed all the male children in Bethlehem and in all that region who were two years old or under, according to the time which he had ascertained from the wise men. Then was fulfilled what was spoken by the prophet Jeremiah: "A voice was heard in Ramah, wailing and loud lamentation, Rachel weeping for her children; she refused to be consoled, because they were no more."

But when Herod died, behold, an angel of the Lord appeared in a dream to Joseph in Egypt, saying, "Rise, take the child and his mother, and go to the land of Israel, for those who sought the child's life are dead."

And he rose and took the child and his mother, and went to the land of Israel. But when he heard that Archelaus reigned over Judea in place of his father Herod, he was afraid to go there, and being

> *warned in a dream he withdrew to the district of Galilee. And he went and dwelt in a city called Nazareth, that what was spoken by the prophets might be fulfilled, "He shall be called a Nazarene."*

Any time we talk about Joseph, one of the first things that has to be said is that it's almost all *speculation*. For somebody with such an important role in the life of Jesus, we know next to nothing about him.

If we think about Joseph at all, we have a sentimental picture of Jesus at work beside his father's bench, planing a board or pounding a nail or doing something very humble and simple – making an ox yoke, say, or building a footstool.

We have this mental picture of Mary, Jesus and Joseph, all seated around the table in their humble, holy, home, giving thanks to God before meals, and maybe reading a few chapters out of the King James version of the Bible before bed time.

It's a nice picture, and I don't want to make too much fun of it. But it brings up the point I raised a moment ago. Almost everything we say about Joseph, and about how Jesus was brought up, is pure speculation. It's somebody's imagination about how it all must have been.

The early church made up some absolutely incredible legends about Jesus' childhood – how he built a bridge from a rainbow, or shaped clay into birds that flew away. People made these stories up, because they wanted to know how a boy like Jesus, the carpenter's kid, could have grown up into the Messiah of Israel, and the Savior of the world.

Actually, if you look at the Scriptures closely, it doesn't say that Joseph was a carpenter. It says in another passage that he was a ***teknon***, which is a Greek word that can mean "carpenter," but it can also mean "handyman," "jack-of-all-trades" or "craftsman." It can mean "blacksmith,","mason" or "contractor."

So what it boils down to is that Jesus came from a working-class background. Maybe that explains why Jesus got on so well with fishermen and poor people later in life. But we can't really get too much more out of the Scriptures. Anything else, all of our pictures of the Holy Family, are all pure imagination.

While I'm on the subject, let's talk about what else we know about Joseph. Joseph is only mentioned a few times in the gospels, mostly around the Nativity. Since Joseph isn't on the scene during Jesus' ministry, and Mary is, people tend to assume that Joseph died young.

In fact, some writers, especially in the Roman Catholic tradition, take their speculation a step farther. They want to keep Mary from having more than one child, and there are references about Jesus' brothers in the Bible. So they say that Joseph was an older man, a widower with children from a first marriage, who married Mary and then died when Jesus was still in his teens. That way, Jesus can still be Mary's only child.

It's a nice idea, and maybe it's true, but again, it's all speculation.

What does stand out from the Christmas story, which is not speculation, is something we often overlook. And that's that Joseph, whatever else he might have been, was a dreamer. Did you ever notice that? In this morning's gospel, what we have is a picture of Joseph as a person who *dreamed*.

The first time we see this, is when Joseph discovered that Mary was pregnant. They were formally engaged, but not yet married. And it says that "Joseph, who was a good [or just, or righteous] man, was unwilling to expose her to public disgrace, and planned to dismiss Mary quietly . . ."

That's our first indication of what kind of person Joseph is. Honorable, maybe conventional, but kind. He was unwilling to put his fiancé to shame, even though he thought she had betrayed their agreement.

And then, he had a dream. An angel appeared to Joseph in a dream, and told him that it was all right for him and Mary to be married, because the child was from God. And when Joseph woke up, it says, he did what he had been told. He took Mary to be his wife, in the face of all the public censure which I'm sure would have been present, and gave the child the name which had been told to him in the dream.

Then we read about the wise men, which is where we usually spend most of our time when we read this story. But after the wise men left, Joseph had another dream. This time, the angel warned Joseph to take his young family and run away to Egypt. The anger and paranoia of the king was a threat to their lives.

Joseph got up in the middle of the night, and was well on the way by daybreak. They stayed in Egypt, in a land where they were strangers, for a year or two until it was safe to come back.

Because Joseph was obedient to his dream, because he *acted* on what the angel told him, Jesus' life was saved. And possibly Mary's and Joseph's lives as well.

Then Joseph has a third dream: "Get up, take the child and his mother and go to the land of Israel, for those who were seeking the child's life are dead. . ."

And so they return, but then Joseph has a fourth dream, which said that it was too dangerous to live nearby to Jerusalem, because Herod's son was in power. So they moved again, this time to Nazareth, a little town way off in the sticks. And there Joseph settled, worked, and raised his family, and is heard from only once or twice again.

If we want to look at Joseph, strictly from the point of view of what is actually said in Scripture, we would have to say that on the record, there is a lot more evidence that Joseph was a dreamer, than that he was a carpenter.

Joseph might have been a carpenter, just as a way to put bread on the table. The Jews of that day required every man to know a trade. Even the greatest rabbis were trained that way. The apostle Paul, who was trained in the Law, was also a tentmaker. Joseph's carpentry might have been kind of a sideline, a sort of a fall-back skill that he used when times were tough.

But from the evidence, on four widely-separated occasions, Joseph had important dreams – and he *acted* on them. Joseph wasn't a daydreamer. He wasn't indulging in fantasies, or imagining things to himself. He recognized those few important times when his dreams came straight from God, and he acted on them.

People talk about Joseph the carpenter, and I've heard all sorts of sermons about how he must have taught Jesus things like honesty and craftsmanship and attention to detail and things like that. I'm sure that many of us have heard about how Jesus' famous line about "take My yoke upon you, and learn from Me", must have come from his childhood experience making ox yokes with his father, Joseph, in the carpentry shop. But you almost never hear people talk about Joseph the *dreamer*, or about how Joseph might have influenced Jesus in that way.

I want to be careful not to speculate too far in a different direction. But it seems fair to me that Joseph the dreamer might have had more of an impact on Jesus than Joseph the carpenter ever managed to have.

First, notice that Joseph's dreams weren't *selfish* dreams. They didn't express his personal ambition. All of the instructions in Joseph's dreams were on behalf of others – on behalf of Mary, or on behalf of the child, Jesus. And in the background, maybe there's a sense that his dreams were on behalf of other people – God's people, God's purpose and plan.

It's normal enough for us to have selfish dreams, or personal dreams. But it takes a kind of integrity to have dreams of power for others.

Second, notice how Joseph's dreams were rooted and woven in *history*. Even if you disregard all of the comments in the Scriptures about how "this-and-such was done to fulfill the saying of the prophet so-and-so," Joseph had to have known that there were echoes and parallels in what he was being told in his dreams.

To flee to Egypt and then return from Egypt *had* to have reminded Joseph of the story of the Exodus. It had to have reminded him of Moses, the great deliverer of the people of Israel. Even if nobody else thought about it, Joseph had to have looked down at the little boy in his arms, and wondered if he would be a second Moses, who in God's name would help to bring freedom and purpose to the people.

Third, if you can believe that Joseph taught Jesus anything about carpentry, you can even better believe that Joseph taught Jesus something about *obedience* to the leading of God. He must have taught Jesus something about following the Spirit, about walking through fear, about finding God's presence in the midst of ordinary and confusing events. Because, on the record, that's the kind of life that Joseph himself actually led.

We're used to saying that Joseph must have had a great influence on Jesus' later life. But we may not realize just how great that influence might have been.

It says in the gospels that "Jesus spoke as one in authority," and not as ordinary people. Part of that authority he found on his own. But part of that authority he must have learned from Mary and Joseph, who each in their own day had listened to angels and dreams, and who had trusted God's power, and obeyed.

I'm not sure that I want to come right out and say that we should blindly follow whatever dreams come to us, starting when we lay our heads down on our pillows this evening. But I guess I want to hint that Joseph was on the right track.

I think that dreams come to people who are ready to receive them. I think that if we can learn to dream – if we can receive the dreams that God plants in us, and ponder them, and act on them – then I think we may come closer to following God.

God speaks to us through the Scriptures. And God speaks to us through the Holy Spirit, and through the examples of the lives of others who have followed in faith where God led them. But the story of Joseph reminds us that God also sometimes speaks in dreams, as well.

Most of us get up in the morning, and we say, "Eh, it was just a dream." And we go on about our business. Joseph got up and he said, "Lead, and I follow. . ."

We could all do a lot worse than imitate Joseph, the dreamer.

VI

Questions

The story this time is about when Jesus was a little boy.

It's a very important story. Because this is the only place in the whole Bible where we have any information about Jesus' growing up.

For most famous people in history, we have much more information about their childhood. For any famous person today, we would have a lengthy biography. If someone is a famous actor, or a business person, or a politician, we would know all about the way they grew up, with interviews from every neighbor, teacher and playmate.

But we know very little about Jesus. We know much more about the president of the United States than we know about Jesus. And which person is more important? Who has made a more important and lasting contribution to history?

In the last meditation, we talked about Jesus' adoptive father, Joseph. You'll remember that I said we know almost nothing about Joseph. He's only mentioned a couple of times, and we have almost no details. All that we really know about Joseph is that he worked with his hands, and that he was a dreamer.

Here, we're faced with the same situation. We know next to nothing about Jesus' childhood. All the years that he spent growing up. Listening. Learning. Reflecting. Praying. Discovering.

The only glimpse that we have of those formative years, is in this Bible reading.

Luke 2:41-52

Now his parents went to Jerusalem every year at the feast of the Passover. And when he was twelve years old, they went up according to custom; and when the feast was ended, as they were returning, the boy Jesus stayed behind in Jerusalem. His parents did not know it, but supposing him to be in the company they went a day's journey, and they sought him among their kinsfolk and acquaintances; and when they did not find him, they returned to Jerusalem, seeking him.

After three days they found him in the temple, sitting among the teachers, listening to them and asking them questions; and all who heard him were amazed at his understanding and his answers.

And when they saw him they were astonished; and his mother said to him, "Son, why have you treated us so? Behold, your father and I have been looking for you anxiously."

And he said to them, "How is it that you sought me? Did you not know that I must be in my Father's house?"

And they did not understand the saying which he spoke to them.

And he went down with them and came to Nazareth, and was obedient to them; and his mother kept all these things in her heart. And Jesus increased in wisdom and in stature, and in favor with God and man.

Jesus' parents were religious. They joined their fellow Jews in making a pilgrimage, every year, to the holiest place in the Jewish world, to the Temple.

When I thought about that, it seemed to me that Jesus' family was no different from many other families, in different religions, in different places around the world.

If Jesus' family had been Muslims, they would have taken him with them to Mecca. If Jesus' family had been Roman Catholics, they might have taken him with them on a pilgrimage to Rome. If Jesus' family had been Buddhists, living in Japan, they would have taken him to visit the Buddhist temple at Todai-Ji.

But they were Jews, and so Jesus' family took him with them to the Temple at Jerusalem, the holiest place in the Jewish world, at the holiest time of the Jewish year.

During the festival, religious scholars and religious lawmakers and teachers would come out of their homes and classrooms and offices. They would come to the Temple, and find a corner, or a place on the steps, or an unoccupied place in the court yard.

And they would teach. They would give classes in public and out in the streets. They would hold forums and discussion groups. They would hold question-and-answer sessions for anyone who wanted to come to them. This was so that all the people who had come up to Jerusalem for the festival could learn, and so that they could be excited about questions of religion.

It was probably a way for teachers to attract new students and disciples. Passover was a public festival to bring offerings and to make sacrifices. But it was also a time to meet teachers and to raise questions.

And this is when we get our only glimpse of Jesus' childhood. This is the only time we see Jesus when he was a boy.

Most of what I have heard and read about this story focuses on what I consider to be a trivial part of the narrative – on the anxiety of Jesus' parents.

It's easy for us to understand. All of us have lost someone in a crowd, or we've been separated from our family or friends. We can understand the worry and the anxiousness of Jesus' parents. But that's not what makes this story important.

The other thing people who study this reading talk about, is what Jesus said, when his parents finally found him. "Why were you worrying? Didn't you know that I would be in my Father's house? . . ."

The point here is the relationship that Jesus felt he had with God. Most people think about God as someone who is far off. We can't approach God. God is mysterious and invisible.

Jesus didn't say that. Jesus called God his Father. That doesn't mean that God is a man. It doesn't mean that God is male. It's a *relationship*. It's *closeness*.

The word Jesus used wasn't, "Father, the master of the family, the God who rules everything and frowns at everyone, God the Boss, God the Bad Guy who spanks everyone when he gets home . . ."

The word for "Father" that Jesus used was **abba**. It means, "Daddy." It's the word of love and trust. If you don't like that word, if you have some other name for God, that's fine. We all use the best words that we have to describe God.

Jesus called God, **Abba**. "I was at *Abba's* house . . ." That's the voice of a little boy talking. But it's also the voice of someone who loved and trusted God, who brought God near, and who felt that God wasn't someone to be afraid of.

Anyway, that's what most people talk about, when they read this story. What I wondered about, when I read this story this time, was something completely different. It's something we almost never talk about. It's a detail we almost always miss.

What was Jesus *asking* the teachers at the Temple?

What was it, that he wanted to know?

What *questions* was he asking them?

I wondered about that a lot. And so I spent some time asking other people what they would have asked, if they had been there.

I asked quite a few twelve-year-olds what their questions would have been. I also asked some younger children, and some teen-agers, and some adults. "What questions do you have about God? Here's your chance. What's something which has always bothered you? What kind of social or religious questions have really struck you? What do you wish you really understood?"

It was my personal poll and I thought I would bring it with me to this meditation. Because I think that here, in the story of Jesus, we have an opportunity to ask some of those questions.

Nothing is out of line. No question is a stupid question. Everyone shares this sense of wanting to know, and feeling that God has the answers, or at least feeling that God can take us a few more steps along the way.

The kind of questions people shared with me varied. They were all different. Some people asked, "What's going to happen to me when I die?" That's a good one. We all want to know that.

Other people asked, "Why do people suffer? Why are there things like diseases, and wars, and injustices in the world? Tell me, why. I really want to know . . ."

One young person asked, "What if it's all a joke? What if everything we do about religion is just kidding ourselves? What if there's nothing? What if God doesn't exist? What are we doing here, then? . . ."

There's really something liberating about questions. If it's all right to ask anything, if no question is truly improper or impolite or out of line, the whole world opens up in front of us.

I'm not offering answers. I'm not sure how much the church is supposed to be in the answering business. I think one of the most important things this story says, is that it's always OK to ask questions. Because even Jesus asked them.

The church, to me, is a place where it's all right for people to ask *any* question. Any question at all, whether it's philosophical, or practical. Whether it has to do with the beginning and end of the universe, or whether it's about why a child is scared in the middle of the night. And anything in between.

Church needs to be a safe place to ask questions. To ask ourselves. To ask each other. To ask God. Anyone can ask. Children. Teenagers. College and graduate students. Couples. Singles. Anyone. This is a safe place to ask.

One particular category of questions that I picked up a lot during my survey, were questions which have to do with things we see in life around us. A lot of people asked me,

"Why do people in such-and-such a situation act like this? Why are people's lives this way? What does God think about what I'm seeing?"

Why do people who are smart or pretty or handsome get all the attention? Shouldn't we be friends, even if we're not that way?

Why do people who have lived good lives, who have never hurt anyone, who have never done anything to deserve illness, get cancer?

Why should people be treated badly, because their skin is a different color? Why should generations of them have to suffer?

When we see things, we're going to ask questions. That's the way people are. All of our religious faith, and all of our human effort, comes back to questions like *"Why?," "Who?," "What?," "Where?,"* and *"When?"*

That's why this story is important, because that it's where get our first glimpse of Jesus, as a person who *asked questions.*

I don't think that people just magically grow up. I think we grow through the experiences we have, from what our families pass on to us, from our teachers, through the social conditions around us. People grow up through all these things. And I think Jesus was no different in that way.

And I still want to know, what questions Jesus asked, when he sat with the teachers in the Temple.

I think we can make a guess at what Jesus asked, because we know some of the things that Jesus taught, later on. We can try to "fill in the missing pieces" by looking at what Jesus said later.

For example: since Jesus was in the Temple, with people coming and going all around him, maybe one of the things he asked was, "What should people do, when they pray?"

It's a natural enough question. You see people coming to worship. They all seem to be praying. Some people even argue about what form of prayer is best. "What should people do, when they pray?"

Any of us could have asked that. And when Jesus asked it, maybe because he felt so close to God, the answer he came up with was to pray, "*Abba*, you live in heaven. May we remember that you are holy. May your kingdom be here on earth, and may what you want be what really happens. Give us what we need each day. Forgive us for what we have done wrong to you, as we forgive our brothers and sisters. Do not let us be tested beyond our ability. Deliver us from evil. The kingdom, and the power, and the glory belong to you. Amen. . ."

I think Jesus' teaching on the Lord's Prayer begins right here, when Jesus was asking questions in the Temple.

Or take another example: as Jesus watched people coming in, he saw that many of them brought gifts. People brought money and sacrifices.

And as Jesus watched, he must have noticed that some people brought more money, or bigger sacrificial gifts, than others. People who were rich brought big gifts. People who were poor brought smaller gifts. People who give more, naturally get more attention. Lots of people like to have a fuss made over them.

At the same time, people who bring big gifts may not be good people. People can give huge amounts of money, and still not learn the basic lessons about how to live. Maybe when Jesus was a boy in the Temple, was when he first thought about what he taught later, when he said, "God desires mercy, and not sacrifices. . ." (Matthew 12:7; *see* Hosea 6:6)

Or maybe Jesus, when he was a boy, looked around the Temple and saw the crowds and the commotion there. And maybe he went home and read in the prophets, "I hate, I despise your feasts, and I take no delight in your solemn assemblies. Even though you offer me burnt offerings, I will not accept them . . . Take away the noise of your songs, I will not listen to your musical instruments. But let justice roll down like waters, and righteousness like an ever-flowing stream. . ." (Amos 5:21-24)

We learn, as children, the lessons we live for the rest of our lives. And the questions that we ask as children don't go away.

I'm sure that Jesus, as a boy, saw plenty of religious violence. There were plenty of people in Jesus' day, who said that it was all right to hate other people, and to kill other people, and that they would have God's blessing if they did. It could be that Jesus even heard people teaching that, in the Temple. The Jews, along with every other religion, have had their share of religious violence.

Maybe it was what Jesus saw as a boy that later made him tell his friend, Peter, ""Put your sword back into its place; for all who take the sword will perish by the sword . . ." (Matthew 26:52)

Or maybe the violence that he saw is what made Jesus say, "My kingship is not of this world; if my kingship were of this world, my servants would fight, that I might not be handed over to the Jews; but my kingship is not from the world . . ." (John 18:36)

Or just to give one last example: maybe Jesus heard people asking questions about their homes, about their money, or about their income and possessions. Children hear grown-ups talking about that sort of thing. We can't hide those kind of worries from our children.

Maybe it was when Jesus was a child that he started asking, "Why do you worry so much about what you eat, or drink, or wear? Isn't your life more than food? Isn't your body more than clothing? Look at the birds; they don't plant or harvest or build barns, but *Abba* feeds them. Look at the flowers: they don't work or weave cloth, but even King Solomon didn't dress more beautifully than them. God knows what we need. The first thing to do is to search for God's kingdom, and to search for how to be completely good. Everything else will be taken care of . . ." (author's paraphrase; *see* Matthew 6:25-33)

The questions we ask, lead us to the faith that we have. The questions which really matter to us, are the ones which God wants to answer. Anyone can ask them. Because honest questions, faithfully and persistently asked, always lead us home to God.